Trekking in Nepal

A personal story and practical guide

David Crawford

ISBN: 9781973310709

CONTENTS

Introduction

In October 2017, I went trekking in Nepal. Over 18 days, with eight people I had never met before, I climbed three high passes, summited two mountains and visited Everest Base Camp. This book is a personal account of my journey, advice on preparation and practical tips.

Authors often give their reasons for writing a book in ambitious terms such as sharing knowledge or adding to the sum of human happiness. My motivation is more prosaic and self-indulgent. I wrote a blog whilst on my trip to keep family and friends informed about my adventure; and to provide a diary for myself to capture those precious moments that so quickly get lost during the course of a challenging and exciting trip. People were kind enough to say they had enjoyed reading the blog and sharing my journey from the comfort of their armchairs. So the seed was planted to offer it to a wider audience. But essentially, I am writing this book because I want to record my memories.

The blog forms the central part of the book. This was written contemporaneously onto my phone each night of the trip as I snuggled into my sleeping bag before going to sleep. It is reproduced in this book with minimal editing, still in its raw and immediate form. Hopefully what it lacks in literary style is compensated for by capturing the energy and immediacy of reporting nightly from the mountains.

The blog is preceded by some background information about myself, my motivation for embarking on the trek and things to think about before you go; and followed by practical advice and suggestions for trekkers contemplating a similar trip. It is not intended to replace far more comprehensive guides which are available, such as 'Lonely Planet Trekking in the Nepal Himalaya' or 'The Rough Guide to Nepal'. I do not lay claim to be an expert, but sometimes a simple, lay narrative can be more useful and entertaining than the overly detailed information found in these more heavyweight books.

The Trek

There are two main areas for trekking in Nepal: the Everest region in the east and the Annapurna region in the west. In either case you will fly into Kathmandu before flying on to Lukla (for Everest) or Pokhara (for Annapurna).

Everest is iconic, the treks are at higher altitude and you are surrounded by world famous peaks towering to over 8000m; but it is crowded in peak season. Annapurna is more diverse, less taxing physically, at lower altitude and offers greater scenic variety. I plumped for Everest for the unmissable opportunity to see the highest mountain in the world.

But I prevaricated for many months over whether to visit Everest Base Camp (EBC) or travel elsewhere in the Everest region. EBC simply because it **is** EBC. It's where everybody goes and was voted the number one trek by readers of an outdoor magazine. But elsewhere **because** it's where everybody goes, has a reputation for being crowded and litter strewn, and there are more remote and beautiful places nearby.

In the end I solved my dilemma by deciding to do both. EBC so I could tick it off my bucket list; but also three high passes - Kongma La (5500m), Cho La (5420m) and Renjo La (5400m) - and two summits - Kala Pattar (5545m) and Gokyo Ri (5483m) to get away from the crowds and see areas beyond EBC. It was 18 days of trekking, much of it above 5000m.

Having completed the trek, I can say this was absolutely the correct decision for me. EBC in many ways was a disappointment and anti-climax (though pleasingly it was not litter strewn). I am glad I have seen it, but the rest of the trek was the best.

The route is shown in the map on the next page. It started at Lukla and headed north to Namche Bazaar. We circled anti-clockwise, following the main EBC route until Dingboche where we diverted from this route to cross Kongma La before picking up the main route again at Lobuche. From here we trekked to EBC and Gorak Shep, summited Kala Patter and returned to Lobuche. Next we diverted off the main route again, which was heading back to Namche Bazaar, and crossed Cho La, summited Gokyo peak and crossed Renjo La before rejoining the crowds at Namche Bazaar. From here it was back to Lukla.

My general comments and advice can apply to trekking anywhere, but as my trek was in the Everest region all the more specific details such as flying from Kathmandu into Lukla and the towns and villages visited on the trek, apply only to the Everest region. Most people trek to Everest Base Camp and return, typically taking about 13 days. This, after all, is the location from where so many summit attempts have set off, hence its popularity. It is etched into the consciousness of any person with an interest in the outdoors. But my trek took in far more than just EBC.

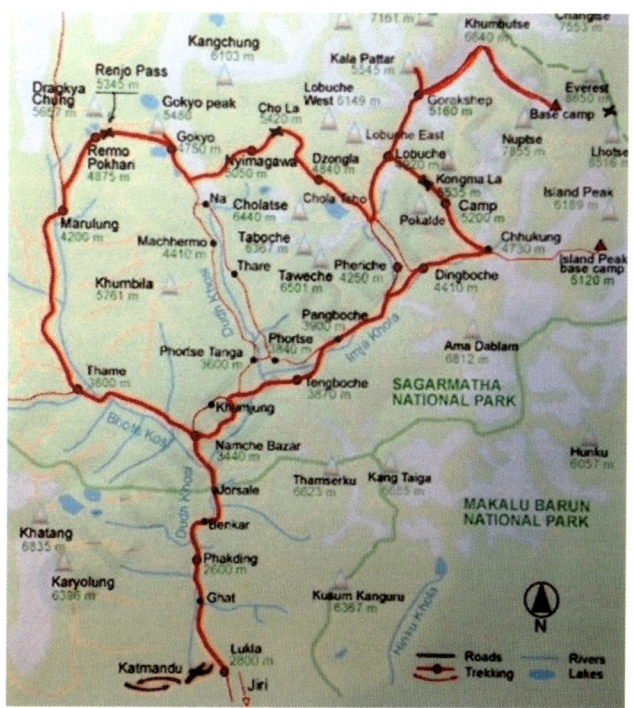

The detailed itinerary is below:

Day 1   Fly Kathmandu to Lukla (2800m) and trek to Ghat (2530m)

Day 2   Trek to Monjo (2850m)

Day 3   Trek to Namche Bazaar (3440m)

Day 4   Rest day at Namche Bazaar. Acclimatisation walks to Everest View Hotel and the village of Khumjung

Day 5   Trek to Deboche (3770m)

Day 6   Trek to Dingboche (4360m)

Day 7   Rest day at Dingboche. Acclimatisation walk above the village

Day 8   Trek to the base of Kongma La. Wilderness camp at 4800m

Day 9   Cross Kongma La (5500m) and trek to Lobuche (4930m)

Day 10   Trek to Gorak Shep for lunch. Continue to EBC and return to Gorak Shep (5288m)

Day 11   Ascend Kala Pattar (5545m) and trek to Lobuche (4930m)

Day 12   Trek to Dzongla (4843m)

Day 13   Cross Cho La (5420m) and trek to Thagnak (4700m)
Day 14   Trek to Gokyo (4800m)
Day 15   Ascend Gokyo Ri (5483m) and trek to base of Renjo La.
         Wilderness camp at 5130m
Day 16   Cross Renjo La (5400m) and trek to Taranga (4000m)
Day 17   Trek to Namche Bazaar (3440m)
Day 18   Trek to Lukla (2880m)
Day 19   Fly to Kathmandu

Before you Go

Fitness

I was 67 at the time of the trip and had concerns beforehand about whether I would be up to the challenge. I had expected to be by far the oldest on the trek, and did not want to let down my younger and fitter fellow trekkers.

I had telephoned the tour operator before booking to enquire about how physically challenging the trek would be. He repeated the advice and information in the brochure, to the effect that it is graded 7, the highest grade for a trek (higher grades up to 10 being classed as mountaineering). I then disclosed my age as 67, and I heard an intake of breath at the other end of the line, followed by the observation that people in their fifties have completed the trek! Undeterred I went for it.

In the event, I need not have worried. I was indeed the oldest in our group of nine, but only by one year. The average age of our group was 60, something of which we were all proud. This was not a special trip aimed at older trekkers, just a normal mixed bag of people, about whom more later. But we were all fit and well-motivated. A group of younger people, on the identical trip and starting just one day behind us, had two members helicoptered out within the first five days. So perhaps younger people are over-confident and think they can just turn up. How hard can it be? Well the answer is tough.

I keep myself fit and am not overweight. I run regularly, having run 18 marathons, and secured a 'good for age' entry to the London marathon for 2017. (Unfortunately postponed to 2018 because of a broken ankle in a skiing accident.) So I am probably fitter than average for a 67 year old, but by no means a super athlete or extreme fitness fanatic. As preparation, I went to the gym regularly for five months before the trip for general strength and fitness, and it paid off. My knees often give me problems if I do long runs or steep downhill walking. But in Nepal I did not suffer at all. I attribute this to the sessions in the gym, five or six times a week. So my advice is get fit. You will enjoy the trip more and be more likely to complete it without delaying your fellow trekkers. It will not protect you against altitude sickness, but you will cope far better with the physical exertions of trekking on steep and rough terrain at altitude.

If you have not previously done any significant walking or trekking, then I would not start with Nepal. Try out some hills in the UK first and see how you fare. I was not a novice walker, trekker or camper. I have always enjoyed the outdoors, dating back to my early years camping with the Scouts, and as an adult running, skiing, sailing and hill walking. At the time of the trek I was over half way through completing the 214 Wainwright peaks in the Lake District. These are the fells described in Alfred Wainwright's seven pictorial guides to the Lake District. They are not as high or as challenging as the mountains of Nepal, but provide valuable hill walking practice. I have also completed the 192 mile Coast to Coast walk from the west coast to east coast of England. And the 96 mile West Highland Way in Scotland from the edge of Glasgow to Fort William. (Though did skip the first stage, starting instead on the bank of Loch Lomond.)

However, my biggest trek before Nepal was to Kilimanjaro, the highest mountain in Africa. It is 5895 metres high, which is higher than Everest

Base camp, or indeed any of the peaks or summits on the trek in Nepal. We started the summit ascent at midnight and the temperature was minus 10°C. So in these respects, Kilimanjaro was more challenging than anything faced in Nepal - higher, colder and in the dark. However, the final ascent from Barafu at 4645m to the summit and back down was all in one day, indeed up and down within 12 hours, so little time was spent at the highest altitude.

This contrasts with the trek in Nepal where we were at around 5000m or above for some 10 consecutive days. Also the total trek lasted 18 days compared with just eight for Kilimanjaro; and the walking in Nepal was often harder and more sustained, especially crossing the high passes. Nevertheless, the Kilimanjaro trek was a good introduction to walking at high altitude and whetted my appetite for the greater challenge offered by Nepal.

However, do not be intimidated if you are not a marathon runner or have not trekked at altitude. All of our group were fit, but not all had experience at altitude nor had been lifelong walkers. Fitness and motivation are essential, but you do not need to be an experienced mountaineer. Use your level of experience and confidence to guide you in deciding how best to organise the trek.

Trekking Options

There are three main trekking options to consider if you are planning a trip to Nepal. The first, and the one I chose, is to go with a well-established tour company. I travelled with World Expeditions, but there are others such as Exodus and Explore. The benefits of booking with one of these large, international tour operators is that everything is organised for you. You are buying peace of mind and the reassurance that you will be well looked after and taken care of if anything goes wrong.

Also, most of the larger companies now promote ethical tourism practices and you should check on this before booking. The porters should be paid the Union-agreed wage, not expected to carry excessive loads, be properly fed, provided with suitable clothing and accommodation, and given medical care if needed. In addition, they should be insured to provide for their relatives in case of any mishap. Such basic provision might be considered obvious and hardly worthy of comment, but sadly for too long the porters were not properly rewarded or looked after. So make sure any operator you use does follow responsible practices.

They should also be concerned to protect the fragile environment, leave no litter and plough money back into the local economy. Nepal is a poor country and has suffered with natural disasters, such as the earthquake in April 2015 which killed an estimated 9000 people, and political instability. In 2001, the Royal family was massacred by the then heir to the throne. The country needs tourism, but it should be responsible and ethical.

There are downsides if you choose to book your trek with a large company. The obvious one is cost. These businesses have offices to run, glossy brochures to produce, websites to maintain and staff to employ. This all has to be covered in the price of your holiday. Prices vary depending on the length of your trek, but at 2017 prices you can expect to pay around £1600 for a trek to Everest Base Camp, plus flights, insurance, tips and incidental expenses. But you get peace of mind, the security of a large operator, trek with other people and are freed from worry if problems arise, whether medical or practical.

You will have to choose from the routes and dates offered in their brochures, so lose flexibility if you have a specific trek in mind or are restricted to certain dates. Some operators do offer tailor made trips, but for the most part you will be limited to the dates and itineraries in the brochures.

You will be sharing your trek with other people you have never met. This can be a mixed blessing. My group had 9 of us, but numbers can go up to around 15. The other people in your group can be an integral part of making the holiday enjoyable; or be a nightmare. You will be living, walking, eating and possibly sharing a tent with them for the duration. In my group, we all got on well, were of a similar age range, walked at about the same speed and gelled together. But this is not always the case.

Other groups I saw splintered and walked at different paces with minimal interaction or conversation. If you are unfortunate to get a particularly loud or obnoxious person in your group, you are stuck with him or her; there is no escape. If others in your group are unfit or unprepared you will be slowed, and if they need evacuation, your trip may be delayed or disrupted. I witnessed examples of all of these in other groups during my trek, so it is the luck of the draw. Fortunately, most people who embark on a trip of this nature are like-minded and keen to be supportive and friendly.

While on the topic of other group members, there is an issue for solo travellers to consider. Unless you pay a single supplement, you will be sharing with someone of the same gender, but a stranger. The accommodation, whether tents or tea rooms, is not spacious, and you will be with this person for the whole trip; in close confinement. You may make a friend for life, but equally snoring, coughing and other personal habits or idiosyncrasies may drive you to distraction. When you really need a good night's sleep a snorer is not welcome.

I paid a single supplement and it was money well spent. Indeed, others on my trek commented that with hindsight they too would have paid for single accommodation. Not all tour operators offer this option, and some only for the hotel in Kathmandu, not whilst actually on the trek. My advice would be to seek single accommodation throughout if you are a solo traveller. You can go to bed when you like, spread your kit around, get dressed, undressed and washed in peace and enjoy a degree of privacy.

If you are not attracted to a large tour operator, an alternative is to trek entirely independently, either solo or with a few friends of your choosing; but without any guide or porters. I would not recommend this if you are new to trekking, or lack confidence in your abilities or are not an experienced overseas traveller. But people do it, and for the busy, main Everest Base Camp route it is entirely possible. (For the higher level passes and summits which are more remote, I would counsel caution unless highly experienced, but some people do indeed do these routes independently.)

The main base camp route is busy with fellow trekkers, the path is clearly marked, you are unlikely to get lost, and there are tea houses offering food and lodgings along all of the route, though less frequent as you go higher. You can research these in advance in one of the comprehensive guide books.

The obvious advantage of doing it alone is much reduced cost. You need a park permit costing about £20 and can eat and stay at lodges for about £20 per night. So a trip to Everest Base Camp of 12 nights trekking might cost you only £300 if you add in a bit of extra for incidentals. You are also free to travel at your own pace, take stops when you want, follow a route of your own choosing and travel either with companions, or alone. You can meet and mix with other trekkers at the tea houses, which in peak season are buzzing with others mostly all doing the same route.

However, you will be carrying all your own kit, and staying and eating at lodges of varying and sometimes dubious quality. Picking up a tummy bug from food or water is a risk. You will not have any back-up support if you encounter problems. You will have to organise everything such as transfer from your arrival airport in the country, internal flights, supplies, kit, accommodation and eating.

One difficulty, in peak trekking season, can be securing a bed for the night, even if you think you have an advance booking in a tea house. It seems to be a common problem that rooms, even when booked, are given to someone else before you arrive. First come first served appears to be the rule, whatever you might think to the contrary.

If you are travelling with a tour operator, they have far more clout than if you are travelling solo. They are bringing the regular business of large parties throughout the season. The tea houses do not want to upset them. But even so, our guide phoned in advance whenever we were due to be staying at a lodge, and he went ahead to claim the rooms and try and ensure we got the best ones. By contrast, in Dzongla (a remote and small village off the main EBC route) a lone, female, German trekker arrived late afternoon and found her booking in a lodge had been let go. Everywhere in the village was full, she had no tent and it was too far and too late to consider walking on. Fortunately, she was allowed to sleep in the dining room. She was not a lone example, as others recounted similar experiences.

Another regular problem is with the flights between Kathmandu and Lukla being cancelled because of poor visibility or bad weather. In peak season, up to 70 flights a day are scheduled. If there are no flights for a couple of days that is a lot of trekkers either trying to get from Kathmandu to start their trek, or depart from Lukla to catch flights home.

Again, the large tour operators carry weight with the airline (and speak the language) so maximising your chance of getting on a flight, and removing the stress and anxiety of trying to find out what is happening, when flights are likely to resume and how do I get a ticket so I can catch my flight home? The alternative is to take a helicopter (which can fly in 1500m visibility compared with 5000m required for planes). But this is expensive and with many people trying to get in or out they can be hard to book. A tour operator will make strenuous efforts to get clients on board a helicopter if necessary.

But if you like a bit of adventure, are flexible over travel plans and confident in handling such minor inconveniences, then you will enjoy the challenge of organising your own trek and have stories to recount in the pub when you get home.

A compromise between the two extremes of a fully organised trek booked with an operator versus travelling independently, is to book your own private guide and porter(s) and arrange your own trip with them directly. (In fact, this is in effect what the tour operators do, charging you for the privilege. They use local guides to take you on your trek, acting as the intermediary between you the customer and the local provider.) You can arrange this either in advance from the UK or on arrival in Kathmandu.

The benefits and disadvantages fall between the two options already described. A private porter and guide might cost around £500 for an EBC trip, and your food and lodging costs will be as for independent travel, perhaps another £300. So you still end up at about half the cost of a big tour operator, and you have the comfort of a guide if things go wrong and porters to carry your bag. You will only need to carry your daypack.

Within reason, you can request the trek you want to take, on dates of your choosing, decide how fast or slow you want to walk, and can stop for photos, food or drink when you feel like it. Your guide will advise on the quality of the tea houses and which foods it is best to avoid to reduce the risk of food poisoning. If you find your booking is 'bounced' your guide will take responsibility for sorting an alternative; and of course, will speak the language which can be helpful if you encounter problems.

If you book a guide from the UK, visit websites to seek recommendations and look for reviews before deciding. People I spoke to in Nepal who had chosen this option seemed very satisfied with the quality of their guides. Alternatively, you can arrive in Kathmandu, visit the Thamel tourist district and select one of the many agencies offering guides and porters. Agree the price and route and be off the next day. But again, I would recommend doing a Google search beforehand to seek advice and reviews, not just picking one at random.

In the end, the choice is up to you. The safest but most expensive option is with an established tour operator. The boldest and cheapest is travelling completely independently at about a quarter of the cost. Hiring a personal guide and porter is a half way house at about half the cost. (These cost comparisons do not include fixed costs such as flights or insurance, which will be the same whatever option you choose.)

Kit

I will not bother with a detailed kit list as these are readily available elsewhere. If you are travelling with a large tour company they will supply a comprehensive list; if you are travelling independently you should already be familiar with what to take. If not, you should probably not be going independently.

You will need warm clothing for the cold nights and possibly daytimes. Multiple layers are best as this allows flexibility as conditions vary. A Buff or similar neck warmer is invaluable for warmth during the day and for sleeping in at night. It can be worn under a hat for extra warmth, or on its own to protect your head from the sun; and it can be pulled over the nose and mouth to keep out dust.

But during the daytime, in the autumn season at least when I was there, it should be warm and sunny. Shorts, sun-hat, t-shirt and sunglasses were all needed, as well as suncream and lip salve.

Tour operators will either provide or have available for hire items such as a warm sleeping bag, down jacket and sleeping mat (if camping); but you may prefer to take your own. They will also provide a bag for the porters to carry with all your spare clothing and other items, leaving you with only your daypack.

A daypack of 30 to 35 litres is generally recommended, but I would suggest slightly larger, around 40 litres. Although it is only a daypack, you will need to carry warm clothing, wet weather clothing, hat, gloves, Buff, camera, water, food, sun cream, lip salve, sunglasses, phone and personal first aid kit. This can be quite bulky. I would rather have a sack half empty than having to drape clothing over the top.

A word on weight limits for the flight from Kathmandu to Lukla. When I travelled it was only 15kgs for both your main bag to go in the hold and your hand luggage. The kit supplied by my tour operator (bag, sleeping bag, jacket and sleeping mat) weighed 6kgs. So you have only 9kgs left for all your personal gear and clothing. Less than the hand luggage allowance on a European budget airline flight! Overweight luggage was charged at about £2 per kilo, but there is also the possibility, if the plane is overloaded, that your overweight luggage will simply be left for a later flight. So try and stay within the limit.

Fortunately, the security checks at Kathmandu and Lukla airports are far less stringent than for an international airport. You can carry water bottles and your camera through the security screening, thus reducing the weight of your luggage, and wear a couple of extra layers of clothing to be removed once you arrive at your destination. In this way you can get an extra couple of kilos on board.

Nevertheless, even with these additions, 15kgs for your basic luggage is not a lot for an 18 day trek. You will need to pare down to the essentials. I decanted liquid soap and suncream into smaller and lighter containers, reduced my spare clothing, and left behind optional items such as sandals and a book. Gaiters were the only item I took but wished I had left behind as they were not needed.

Items I did not take, but wish I had, were a lightweight clothes line, a flannel and shorts. You will need to wash clothes as you cannot take enough for the full duration of the trek, and drying can be problematic. If you wash when you arrive at your overnight stop, clouds are welling up and temperatures are dropping. So you have a pile of damp washing to carry next day. You can peg a few items to the outside of your rucksack as you walk, but a clothes line offers opportunities to string up inside your tent or room, or leave out in the sun if you arrive at your destination before the clouds have developed. A flannel because washing yourself is tricky as there are no washrooms. So it is usually just a bowl of water in your tent or room. A flannel allows a more thorough body wash, not just hands and face. Finally, shorts for the warmer than expected weather. Zip-offs afford the flexibility of both shorts or full length trousers.

A supply of waterproof stuff sacks (or just supermarket plastic bags) is invaluable. They allow you to keep your clothes and other items sorted, for example into clean and dirty or wet and dry. And a waterproof sack for your sleeping bag in case of wet weather. You do not want to be sleeping in a damp bag when it is below freezing at night.

Cold temperatures drain batteries, so take spare ones for your head torch and keep electrical items, such as your phone or camera, warm if you want them to work in the morning.

However, you do not need to take everything with you from the UK. Indeed this can be a useful way of saving weight for the flight to Lukla. There are plenty of shops in Lukla, Namche Bazaar and all along the way to EBC (though more sparse as you gain altitude). They sell a wide range of essentials such as soap, hand sanitiser, toilet paper, toothbrushes, tissues, batteries, sun cream, chocolate bars and drinks; as well as clothing, maps, sunglasses, hats, gloves, walking poles etc. Many of the clothing items have branded names on them, but don't be fooled. Look at the prices. You will not be getting an Arc'Teryx jacket for £25! But if you accept it is a jacket, and at a good price and it meets your need for the trek, then buy it. You can leave it for the porters at the end if you don't want to take it home.

The price of goods rises as you ascend. So a bottle of water in Kathmandu was 30NPR, 100NPR in Namche and 150NPR closer to EBC. But this is not unreasonable when you remember everything has to be carried up the mountain by yak or human. But it is worth buying lower down rather than waiting to ascend, unless you don't want to carry it, in which case pay the premium.

Walking poles are a topic of discussion and disagreement. I used to be rather snooty about them. This was based on seeing organised groups of 'ramblers' in the Lake District walking along a flat, paved path by the shore of a Lake, all walking with their poles - click, click, click. It seemed more of an affectation than an aid to walking.

But I was converted (though still not for flat walking on tarmac) when I trekked up Kilimanjaro, and have since used them regularly in the Lakes. On steep ascents and descents they add stability, take the strain off the knees and give extra support and leverage. But other people hold opposing views and believe they are just something extra to carry, an encumbrance in some situations and can lead you to rely too much on the poles, risking a fall if the poles slip. There is also a view that they leave holes in soft ground and scratch rocks, damaging the environment. So you must decide. But I would advise you to at least try them out on steep ground, up and down, before a big trek to Nepal because you may find them a great help.

However, on flattish ground they are not necessary, and on very steep ascents or descents, where you need to use your hands for extra grip or stability, they become a liability. One sees people with sticks flailing as they use their hands for support whilst scrambling up rocks. So you need to be able to stow and retrieve your poles as the terrain varies. Osprey sacks have a system which allows poles to be stowed without removing the pack. This is a great boon. Most other packs have loops on the rear of the pack, necessitating its removal to get at your poles.

Visa

You will need a tourist visa for either 15 or 30 days costing £20 or £35 respectively. This can be obtained in advance from the Nepalese Embassy or on arrival at Tribhuvan (Kathmandu) airport. You should download, print-off and complete the application form in advance (though they are also given out on the plane) and take a passport photo with you. You take these to a desk where you pay your fee (in Sterling or US dollars) and are given a receipt, and then proceed to the immigration desks where you will get a visa stamp in your passport.

If you have an electronic passport there are now visa registration machines in the immigration hall which, after inserting your passport, will automatically fill out the visa form for you. But as you will see from my Blog, I had difficulties with these. The first machine would not read my passport and I was directed to another machine. Eventually I completed the process, which includes taking your photograph, and the machine issued a receipt which I took to the payment desk before proceeding to the immigration desks. But the officer immediately requested a paper form and a photo. So I don't understand what the electronic machine actually achieved. Luckily I had taken a completed form and photo as well, so he issued my visa. But based on my experience, I would not bother with the electronic machines, and instead suggest you just have the paper form completed in advance with a photo and go straight to the payment desk and then immigration desks.

Currency

The currency is the Nepalese rupee. When I travelled in October 2017 the exchange rate was about 135NPR to the pound. (All guide prices in this book are based on this, but may be subject to change.) You cannot buy rupees in the UK, nor exchange them on your return. I recommend you take all your currency needs in pounds

Sterling. There are currency exchange shops in all the main towns such as Kathmandu and Namche Bazaar, and the rate stayed much the same even higher up the mountain. Larger hotels in Kathmandu also offer exchange, though at a slightly less advantageous rate.

The alternative to taking a lot of cash is to take a debit card and use ATMs. These can be found without difficulty in the larger towns, but are often not working, so taking cash is a more certain option. Some restaurants and hotels accept credit cards, but not the smaller and more remote tea houses.

The Blog

I kept an online diary throughout my trek, starting with a couple of posts two weeks before departure and then recording each day's activities once on the trek. The online Blog can be found at:

www.nepal623.wordpress.com

Most of it was written at night, in my sleeping bag, on my phone by the light of my head torch. It is reproduced in its original form, apart from minor corrections such as spelling errors, to capture the excitement and challenges of the trek. The days are numbered from Day one of the trek.

Welcome to my Blog

It is ten days until I depart on a trip to Nepal. I will return (hopefully!) 22 days later having completed an 18 day trek to Everest base camp and beyond. Crossing three high Himalayan passes (Kongma La, Cho La and Renjo La) and summiting Kala Pattar (5545m) and Gokyo Ri (5483m). Staying in a mix of campsites and lodges.

This has been in gestation for some years. I was attracted by the romantic allure of Everest Base camp, but had heard that it has become busy, touristy and untidy with litter and discarded summit equipment. Other parts are meant to be more scenic, far less crowded and with more opportunity to meet locals and imbibe the culture. But EBC is iconic. Where all those attempts on the summit have set off. What to do?

So I discussed my dilemma with a consultant from World Expeditions at a travel show (well a salesman really, but consultant sounds more professional) and he said you need to do our 18 day Everest High Passes expedition and you get the best of both. Sign here! So I did. Well, not actually there and then, but you get the idea.

So what's in store? I fly from Manchester via Dubai and Dhaka (in Bangladesh) arriving 21h 10m later in Kathmandu. Exhausted. There is a briefing meeting that evening and the following day is sightseeing before departure on the trek on Friday 6 October. We fly in a twin-engined Otter (don't know what that is, but it sounds small) to Lukla, where we start walking. [Note. In the event the trek left on Thursday 5th, postponing the sightseeing trip until the end.]

From Lukla we trek north to Namche Bazaar, the Sherpa 'capital' of Nepal and then circle anti clockwise to Dingboche and over the Kongma La pass (5500m). We leave the circular route to head towards Everest base camp (4930m) before returning to Lobuche and continuing the circle, crossing the high pass of Cho La (5420). From here on the views are described as magnificent as we walk through a valley of turquoise lakes and glaciers. We cross our third and final high pass, Renjo La (5400m), before starting our gradual descent back to Namche Bazaar and finally Lukla for the flight back to Kathmandu.

I have been getting myself extra fit for the last 6 months with regular trips to the gym, as well as my usual running. But not as much hill walking as I would have hoped as the weather has not been kind when I had plans to get to the Lakes to tackle some hills. It's now too late to do much more. Fingers crossed I have done enough.

I did a trek to Kilimanjaro two years ago, but that was only eight days, not eighteen. And although the summit of Kili is actually higher (5895m) than any point on this trip, the final ascent is up and down in a day, whereas on this trip I will be at 5000m or above for some nine consecutive days. Hopefully I will cope with the altitude, but fitness is no protector. It seems to be the luck of the draw!

I have been sorting out what to take for some weeks now, occupying the spare bedroom with assorted walking and camping gear. The biggest challenge has been getting the weight down. The limit is 15kgs for everything. But on arrival in Kathmandu they provide a bag for the porters to carry, a sleeping bag and liner, a down jacket and sleeping mat, which together weigh 4.5kgs. [Note. It turned out to be 6kgs.] So only 10.5kgs of personal gear including the weight of a rucksack. Which is just about the weight limit for hand luggage with Ryanair. For 18 days! So liquids like soap and suncream have been decanted into smaller plastic bottles; clothing has been discarded; camera bag and toilet bag replaced with lightweight freezer bags; and everything else pared back to a minimum. How many Imodium tablets will I need?

My rather smart travel wallet with tickets, insurance and itinerary etc arrived today, which makes it suddenly seem very real.

I chose World Expeditions (apart from the sales representative doing a good job convincing me this was the trip I wanted) because they have a strong ethical policy for their Sherpas. They pay them the amount agreed with the Labour Union of Nepal, give them three meals a day, provide accommodation on the mountain, proper clothing, first aid and life insurance. (If this seems obvious, many trekking companies don't provide these things.) They also aim to benefit the local economy and safeguard the ecosystem. I will report on my return if they live up to their promises.

Ten days to go.

Departure day minus one

So, after months of planning and weeks of packing and re-packing, finally I leave tomorrow. At last it starts to feel real. Until now, I have known I am going, but it has been hard to really believe it. Now I know this time tomorrow I will be in the air.

It's been a curious week. I was all packed a couple of weeks ago, so there is no last minute panic. It has felt a bit flat, waiting without much to do, and then worrying I might be getting complacent and should be doing something. Like an actor waiting to go on stage and then worrying about forgetting his lines. I saw my climbing group on Monday and my running group on Tuesday, and did a Park Run with some of them on Saturday. Thank you for all their good wishes.

A full family farewell visit at the weekend – son and daughter and spouses and first grandchild, as well as my 98 year old mother – was a wonderful distraction. Today everyone has gone, so it really is last minute packing of things that can't go in till now – phone, glasses, wallet.

Last meal at home tonight, then early departure to Manchester tomorrow for a 10am flight.

Thank you to people following this blog. It is comforting to know that friends and family will be keeping up with my adventure whilst I am thousands of miles from home.

Departure from the UK and arrival in Nepal

A 6.30am start to get to Manchester for the first leg of my three part journey. And it was indeed a journey of three parts. The plane from Manchester was a wide-bodied, double-decker monster with four huge engines. And less than half full. I had four centre seats all to myself. Luxury.

At Dubai I had six hours to kill before boarding the plane to Dhaka in Bangladesh. What a contrast. The plane was still wide-bodied, but absolutely full with Bangladeshi families. I was one of a very few white faces. Queuing does not appear to be in their national character. More of a scrum. People loading oversize luggage into the lockers was chaotic and moving along the plane was a challenge. But finally everyone is settled. Then someone has to be taken off because of being medically unfit to travel.

This delayed take-off for over an hour. And I only originally had under two hours at Dhaka before my next flight, now reduced to less than an hour. So I had my hand-luggage out of the locker before landing, seat belt ready to be unclipped, arm rest up all ready for a quick dash to try and get nearer the door. No chance. As soon as the plane touched down and still travelling at speed along the runway people stand up and start opening the overhead lockers. The cabin crew are yelling 'Sit down!' and being ignored. General mayhem.

When I finally got off, I had to find the check-in desk, as Manchester could not issue a boarding pass for the final flight. So I found the transfer desk, asked to go to the front of the queue and obtained a boarding pass. Phew. Just in time. And then after all this angst, I discovered the flight time had been moved 30 minutes later, so I need not have been in such a panic.

So to flight three – Dhaka to Kathmandu with Bangladeshi airlines. A single aisle old looking plane. But at first, with only about 30 people on board. Great I thought, plenty of room to relax. Till a bus load of young men arrived, all knowing each other (workers going home from Qatar I later discovered). And then another bus load; and another; and then a few more stragglers. The plane was packed full, with the person in front of me reclining his seat for the whole journey.

Finally at Kathmandu airport, I now had to obtain a Visa. An electronic machine scans your passport, takes a photo and you have to fill in your details on a screen. All a bit high tech. It then issues a bit of paper – not a visa – to be taken to a desk where you pay £21 and get two more bits of paper – but still not the visa – and proceed to the immigration desk. Here the immigration officer asks for a paper form and photograph. I explain I used the electronic scanning machine, but no, I have to have a form and a photo (which luckily I had put in my bag just in case). Form completed and photo attached he asked for my boarding card. I still had it, but no, not just for my last completed flight but also the two previous legs of my journey. Why? And I hadn't kept them. Fortunately my baggage reclaim ticket from Manchester convinced him I had indeed travelled from Manchester, and he stamped a visa in my passport. I was in!

Next challenge. Collect my luggage. The conveyor belt had countless large cardboard boxes wrapped in cling film and a cargo net; and even more large, blue-check canvas holdalls also wrapped in cargo nets. Workers returning home. But not an Antler suitcase! I waited and waited. Eventually to my great relief it appeared. All in, my journey had taken 23h45m. And no sleep.

I located my hotel pick-up amongst the maelstrom of taxis, cars and people holding up cards for meeting strangers.

So finally the drive into Kathmandu. Chaotic traffic, a cow lying oblivious in the road with cars and motorbikes swerving round it, dust, noise, vibrancy and people. I've arrived.

Day 1 of the trek

Kathmandu to Ghat

An alarm call at 5am in the hotel is the start of the day. Gear for the trek, weighing no more than 15kgs, has to be downstairs ready for a 6am departure. Stuff not needed on the trek is left at the hotel.

Off to the internal flights airport, teeming with taxis, buses and people in trekking gear carrying rucksacks. If our collective group luggage weighs more than 15kgs per bag, then they may decide to remove a bag, any bag not necessarily the overweight one, and the plane flies without! Luckily we are OK. (We meet another group later in the day who had to pay an excess baggage charge of about £20, but as the offender did not own up, there was much bickering in their group.)

The plane is a tiny propeller driven craft, holding about 20 people in just a single row down each side. Noisy and vibrating. The hostess brings round a tray of sweets to suck and tells us to read the safety card. (None of this 'In the

unlikely event …. etc). I was told I was in charge of the emergency window exit. And we're off.

We fly east towards the foothills of the Himalayas. Over steep hillsides, tiny, scattered villages in the most remote, inaccessible places and then swoop in for a spectacular landing at a tiny, uphill landing strip squeezed into the hill side at Lukla. No margin for error here. The airstrip was built at the instigation of Sir Edmund Hillary to support his work in developing schools and hospitals in the region.

Lukla is a thriving, buzzing, lovely village all thanks to the airstrip and tourists. Small shops, tea rooms (the equivalent of our cafés), guest houses and small hotels are packed into winding streets. Groups of dzopkos (a cross between a cow and a yak) are herded along the streets, used to carry supplies higher up the mountain. (No cars can get up here.) Watch where you step! It all looks so Nepalese. Well of course it would, but it does not disappoint. Fluttering prayer flags, prayer wheels to spin (always clockwise for good luck), friendly people in bright, traditional clothes.

We stop in a tea room for 'black tea'. Which is not bad. And then the trek begins. It is only a couple of hours today to break us in gently, and mostly downhill. We descend from 2800m to 2500m. The hills are steep and forested, the sky blue, the sun shining bright and warm. Trekkers

are heading up and down. Sherpas are carrying loads up and sometimes down. Donkeys and dzopkos pass by us.

And by midday we have arrived at our camp for the night at Ghat. It is a campsite set up for the use of World Expeditions groups on land rented from a local tea house. Tents you can stand up in, a bed with a pillow, toilets and dining room in the tea house. It's almost

Photo © P Read

too comfortable for my liking. Trekking should be camping on the ground in remote areas. I hope this will come later.

Lunch, afternoon tea and dinner all provided, so we can just relax. An early night for a 6am wake up call. And it has started to rain!

Day 2

Ghat to Monjo

The rain had stopped by the morning. Woken at 6am with a cup of black tea then a bowl of hot water for a wash. Luxury! At breakfast learned that one of our group had gone to the toilet in the night and returned to the wrong tent. Went in and grabbed the foot of the person in 'his' bed!

Off by 8am. Walking up a steep-sided wooded valley with a raging, gushing river below. Blue skies, white cotton-wool clouds and it's hot. There are pretty blue and white houses in little groups along the path and even small villages strung along the route. Tourism is their lifeblood

We cross the river three times on long but narrow wire suspension bridges which bounce and sway as you walk and the river thunders below, visible through the metal slats beneath your feet. Donkey trains and dzopko herds pass us on the path carrying large loads. We stop twice at tea houses for drinks.

The Nepalese people are reserved and gracious. It feels a peaceful and harmonious country. No trying to force you to buy anything. The children are well-behaved and polite, as are the dogs. (We were told to zip up our tents at night otherwise a dog might come and join us. And if going to the toilet, look down outside the door as a dog might be sheltering there for warmth!)

And we catch a glimpse of our first snow-covered Himalayan peak. Excitement ripples through the group.

We arrive at our campsite at Monjo. As last night, an established World Expeditions camp with pre-erected tents and a warm and comfortable building for eating. Though the food so far has been a curious mix and not to my liking. Rice and potatoes and bread; vegetable curries; but only a little protein such as tinned tuna or tinned sausages!

An afternoon walk to visit the local village, spin prayer wheels and admire religious symbols painted all over huge boulders.

We visit a school and medical clinic – both small and basic with earthquake damage – then back for 'washy washy' i.e. a bowl of hot water, and afternoon tea

Dinner tonight was another strange mixture of a papadum, bean soup, spaghetti with tomato sauce and Chinese dumplings, followed by semolina!

And so to bed. The group is gelling well. We are all in late 50s or sixties. And I thought I would be with a load of youngies on such a challenging trek. Five Ozzies, a Swede married to one of the Ozzies and three Brits. Tomorrow up at 6am and walking to the Sherpa capital of Nepal.

Day 3

Monjo to Namche Bazaar

Our destination today is Namche Bazaar, the Sherpa capital. We set off at 8am as usual walking through pine trees lining the steep sides of the gushing river valley we have followed for a couple of days. Again we have a couple of wire suspension bridges to cross, but these are now taken in our stride. BUT at the confluence of two rivers feeding into the one we have been following we have to cross the spectacular long and high bridge. And when I say high I mean HIGH as in very high.

We are on the upper bridge. One poor woman crossing in the opposite direction looked petrified and was staring straight ahead with her friend behind with a hand on each shoulder guiding and reassuring her. And there is no alternative but to cross.

Than starts the toughest climb so far up out of the river valley on a steep path with big uneven rocky steps. And the altitude is now 3000m and rising. So shortness of breath is a problem. But our group all keep together and keep going.

By midday we arrive at Namche. Once a small village of just a few houses, the airport at Lukla and the boom in trekking have transformed it into a prosperous tourist town. Souvenir shops, art galleries, cafés, bars and outdoor gear shops. Buzzing with trekkers but a bit tacky and touristy. Even an Irish bar. What is that all about?

Fortunately the traders do not hassle as one wanders around so I peruse at leisure looking for possible souvenirs and presents for when we return here in 14 days towards the end of the trek.

Tomorrow we have a 'rest day' which means we spend another night here to help with acclimatisation, but we will be having a 4 hour walk to a higher altitude before returning to Namche to sleep. Some rest day!

Day 4

Rest day at Namche Bazaar and acclimatisation walks

Part of acclimatisation is to 'walk high sleep low' meaning go up to a higher altitude during the day but return to your start point altitude to sleep. So that is today's rest day.

We trek uphill on a steep track leaving Namche behind. The early morning mist is clearing and we are hoping for good views. After a couple of hours steep climbing above 3500m we emerge from the narrow lowland valleys carved out by rivers to broad glacial ones. The far more gradual rate of climb is welcome. As is the chance to be walking on grass, not stone, across land which could be English moorland or a links golf course. As we walk some towering Himalayan peaks emerge.

We arrive at our destination – Everest View hotel. There is a heliport here (at 3800m) and a proper stone pathway and a grand stone entrance staircase leading to a smart hotel. Japanese tourists visit by helicopter, but cannot cope with the abrupt rise in altitude, so every room has an oxygen cylinder!!

But the views from the terrace are spectacular. We catch our first view of Everest. You might think the clue is in the name, but it all depends on the cloud swirling round the summits. We also see Lhotse and Ama Dablam.

But soon the cloud descends and mist blocks out the sunshine and the temperature drops. Jackets on. Until now it has been t-shirt, sun block and sun hat. We descend by a different route to our camp at Namche.

In the afternoon we have a short ascent to a Sherpa museum, Sherpa cultural centre and Everest expedition centre. Fascinating pictures of Sherpas who have climbed Everest. One 22 times. And the youngest woman at 19. And lovely colourful pictures of Sherpa life.

Tomorrow we continue our ascent.

Day 5

Namche Bazaar to Deboche

Today was a walk of two halves. In the morning, we follow a meandering trail with Everest visible on the horizon ahead of us. The trail is busy with trekkers and yaks. The cry of 'Yak attack' goes up regularly warning us to get close to the side to avoid the big horns.

The trail is so clear and so busy one could easily do the trek (at least so far) without a guide and with no risk of getting lost. There are tea rooms at regular intervals. These are a combination of cafe, restaurant, shop, accommodation, showers and toilet. What more could you need? People just walk the trail and pick somewhere to stay when they are feeling ready for the end of the day. Higher up may be a different story, but here (and we are at 3500m) it is busier than the Lake District.

After 4 hours walking we descend to the river and take lunch on the terrace of a tea room sitting outside in blazing sunshine. It is hot and sunny. T-shirt and sunglasses weather. Glorious.

The afternoon was more challenging. Having descended to the river valley we then had to ascend all the way up on the other side and then some. A two hour relentless uphill slog. Plod, plod, one foot in front of another until we arrive at the monastery village of Thuangboche. The building was destroyed by fire in 1989 and rebuilt with the assistance of Sir Edmund Hillary.

We are allowed in (boots off, smelly socks!) and it is fascinating. A huge Buddha statue at the far end, ornate and richly coloured wall paintings and statues, three rows of benches in the middle, incense burners, robes. Just as we finish looking round, Padam (our Nepalese guide) says do you want to see the ceremony? It starts in 5 minutes. Others seem lukewarm but I say 'Of course'.

So we go back in and assemble in the courtyard as other tourists arrive. A monk unlocks the big padlock on the door and we all traipse in and sit around the side walls. There is an air of expectation. Then three monks come in and sit on the benches, incense burning, and start chanting. Another monk pours each of them a cup of tea whilst they chant. Then they drink their tea and start another chant and their cups are refilled. So not the most exciting spectacle but fascinating to see, hear and smell it. (Incense masking the smell of some 50 pairs of trekkers' sweaty feet.). One is allowed to leave when you wish, and after about 15 minutes our guide signals time to go.

We descend to our overnight campsite. Before dinner we get a demonstration of the portable oxygen chamber. Basically a person size inflatable plastic chamber which is then pumped up to a higher pressure by foot pump and the casualty lies in it for a few hours! Scary. Used twice in
10 years by our guide so let's hope it's not needed.

Day 6

Deboche to Dingboche

Awake to another glorious day. Bright sunshine which lasts all day. Walking in t-shirt and sun hat, as for all the days. The trail is busy with trekkers. It is the start of the peak trekking season with no sense of isolation or being at one with nature, sadly. But we are all in good spirits as we head along a river valley and cross it on another wire suspension bridge. Ama Dablam, one of the highest Himalayan peaks is visible and getting closer all day.

Photo © P Read

We visit the Pangboche monastery, over 300 years old and inside see in a small cupboard behind a glass screen a Yeti scalp and finger bones! Legend says the Yeti helped the founding Lama to meditate, so now its scull is preserved in the monastery.

After lunch we re-cross the river and climb above 4000m which is the tree line. There is a quite sudden change in the landscape and the vegetation. We are now in a wide glacial valley. The walking gets easier. There are no more trees, just bushes and plants. And all the time the big mountains are getting closer.

We arrive at our destination of Dingboche at 4360m. This is a sizeable town based entirely on tourism. Numerous hotels and lodgings, small shops surprisingly well stocked for trekkers, two snooker halls, two bakeries and facilities such as showers and a laundry. It is a bit disappointing to find it so commercialised, but it is their livelihood. But thronging with trekkers.

My blood oxygen level has dropped to 88% (normal is around 98%). But we have an acclimatisation 'rest day' tomorrow so hopefully a chance to adapt.

My solar charger is working well and I am popular with the rest of the group who are plugging in!

Day 7

Rest day at Dingboche and an acclimatisation walk

Today is a rest day. Meaning we stay a second night at the same place (and altitude) to acclimatise.

We wake to low cloud, mist and drizzle. The first bad weather we have had. The morning walk is cancelled, so let me tell you a bit about our group.

There are nine of us. Two couples and five individuals. Five Ozzies, a Swede married to an Ozzie and three Brits. They are a super fit crowd. Two beach life savers; a marathon time of 2.32 and another of 3.15. Long distance cycling and serious trekking. The youngest is 49 and the next youngest 56. I am the oldest at 67 but only one year ahead of the next. A GP (Ozzie equivalent), a psychiatrist, cardiac nurse, retired aircraft engineer, ex-Navy, pharmaceuticals and a picture framer. An eclectic bunch. But we have all gelled really well. Walk at the same pace, stick together as a group and have had some great laughs in the evenings.

This afternoon the sun emerges so we had an acclimatisation walk to get us ready for the big challenges looming.

An amusing story from last night. The friendly camp dog crept into one of the couples' tent. The husband woke in the early hours and saw a pair of eyes staring at him! His wife then started shouting 'Out, get out, go!' And the chap in the next tent thought she was talking to her husband!

Day 8

Dingboche to base of Kongma La

Best day so far. Cold night but woke to clear blue skies, not a cloud to be seen and glorious sunshine.

But the reason it was so good is we have finally lost all the other trekkers. There are a couple of routes to Everest base camp and almost everyone takes the direct route, as that is their final destination. But we divert off to head towards the first of our three high passes – Kongma La. We  *trek in isolation all day, just us and our four Nepalese guides. We see an occasional independent walker but only a handful of these. No groups at all. No tea houses, no shops, no signs of civilisation. Most of the time it is just us and the mountains.*

And what mountains. We are getting close now to the really big peaks. Forget the Alps, the Himalayas are the biggest, highest most impressive peaks ever. And as we get ever higher the views get better still. It is a gentle uphill walk at  *first, followed by a steep ascent to the base of the pass.*

And another reason why it is the best day yet is we are wild camping. All the previous camps have been permanent sites with tents you can stand up in and beds and pillows. But all in neat rows like a military camp or Boy Scouts. Tonight we are proper camping at 5000m on the ground in smaller tents, eating in a mess tent and the toilet is a hole dug in the ground. (With a tent and a toilet seat so we have not abandoned all creature comforts). Our guide tells us once, in a high wind, the tent blew away revealing someone on the seat!!

We are lucky with glorious weather. I am sure it can get very wild up here. We have been warned it will be cold tonight and tomorrow morning. We will be setting off at 6am to try and get over the pass (5500m) before the winds pick up. But it will be cold.

It is a clear night and there are thousands of stars and the Milky Way. But too cold to linger and admire.

Day 9

Cross Kongma La pass to Lobuche

Today was the hardest and highest (5500m) day so far. Wake up call was at 4.45am and it was cold. We departed at 6am heading for Kongma La pass. The first of our high passes. But we were lucky with the weather. As the sun rose we were walking in sunshine with no wind, and quickly warmed up and started stripping off multiple layers.

It was hard walking. Uphill relentlessly for some 3.5 hours. And at that altitude one is instantly breathless.

But the scenery is stunning and we are still virtually alone. Just the very occasional independent trekker. As we get higher so the views get more spectacular.

Eventually we sight a line of prayer flags strung across the high point of the pass. We have arrived.

Weather is still glorious, and no wind, so we linger and take photos including a group photo which everyone wants on their own camera necessitating a rigmarole of cameras being passed to guides and instructions being shouted.

We are now overlooking the Khumbu glacier which leads up to Everest, but we cannot see the mountain as it is further round.

Then the descent begins. Another relentless slog, but now downhill over rocks and scree. My knees are standing up well to the pounding. Some in the group are less confident.

Photo © P Read

Finally after 1.5 hours we arrive at our lunch spot just before the Khumbu glacier. It is a picnic, and in the warm sun after an early start we laze out and even grab a brief power nap.

Now to the crossing of the Khumbu glacier. If it conjures up images of beautiful ice, forget it. The ice is hidden under tons of boulders and scree slowly being carried down the valley by the underlying glacier.

We have to ascend a steep and rocky slope which is the side of the glacier. And when we reach the top the sight that greets us is unbelievable. It is as if a giant has just collected boulders of all sizes from huge boulders to sandy dust and strewn them in massive piles and heaps and then shuffled the whole lot up into chaos. In a few places the underlying glacier is visible and there are some lakes and pools of water, but not attractive. And it is perhaps half a mile wide.

The challenge for our guides is to find a route across. Because it is constantly changing and moving it is never the same. And it is a challenge. They scout ahead looking for crossing points. We scramble

over boulders, up and down scree slopes and cross rivulets of water on precarious sometimes wobbly stones. Our guides say it is much worse than usual. On the way across one of our group has a lucky escape. He slips and tumbles a few metres down the rocky slope, and in so doing dislodges a large boulder which is heading towards him. He moves his leg out of the way just in time and is unhurt. But a close shave.

Finally we complete the crossing and have to descend down the slope on the far side of the glacier to our destination for the night – Lobuche.

It is a shanty town on the Everest Base Camp route. We are now well and truly back on the main route to EBC and back to crowds of trekkers. We are staying in Mother Earth Lodge! But forget images of ski lodges or Canadian Rocky Mountain lodges. It is a glorified hostel. Packed out. Our rooms are booked months in advance but the guide had been phoning every day to confirm because they can just re-let the rooms it is so busy. Still we are sleeping inside, albeit in the most basic of rooms. But the main dining room has a warm fire which can't be bad.

Tomorrow we go to EBC. Along with everyone else!

Day 10

Lobuche to Everest Base Camp and return to Gorak Shep

The 'lodge' was quiet last night despite housing 100 trekkers. You'd think one group might have been noisy. And the walls are so thin I can hear everything the Japanese couple next door are saying and even them zipping up their sleeping bags! But fortunately everyone is early to bed and early to rise.

A story from last night. The rooms have a bolt on the outside which can be locked with a padlock. But it can be slid across to be closed by anyone. One of our group got up for a pee in the night and found his bolt locked on the outside. He had to bang on the paper thin walls till another of our group came to the rescue. And he was bursting to go!

5am wake-up call with a cup of black tea then a bowl of hot water for 'washy washy'. We set off at 7am. The plan is to trek about four hours to Gorak Shep, where we are staying the night, have lunch there and dump *our bags, then in the afternoon continue to EBC and return. The trail is just a continuous line of trekkers heading up, and then later in the morning coming down for those that started their ascent from Gorak Shep and are now returning. And the trail is narrow in places, so very congested at times. But it is another glorious sunny day with blue skies.*

The lodge at Gorak Shep is less hectic than last night but my room is a cubicle. I can touch both walls with my arms outstretched! The toilets are called Rest Rooms, but they do have an incense stick burning in them!

After lunch we depart for EBC. Some things in life exceed expectation and others disappoint. EBC is in the below expectations category. We trek along a rocky path for a couple of hours following the path of the Khumbu glacier we crossed with such difficulty yesterday. Then we see EBC close to the bottom of the Khumbu icefall which is the start of most Everest ascents. But the only way you would know is the line of trekkers like ants all heading there. It is perched on a rocky moraine at the edge of the glacier. There are no tents as it is not the climbing season. The terrain is rough, uneven, hostile.

EBC is upper left

When we arrived there were some strings of prayer flags, a sign written in paint on a rock saying it was EBC, and scores of trekkers. And that's it.

Anyway, it is a tick off the bucket list. And we had a group photo and took lots of pictures. And the sight of the Khumbu icefall cascading down into the glacier was impressive (and scary if you thought of crossing it) and the tip of Everest is just visible.

EBC is bottom centre

We return to our lodge at Gorak Shep. It is a small collection of single storey buildings purely for trekkers. Our accommodation is better than last night and the food is better, but it is packed. We were told to take our room keys on the walk to EBC otherwise they might re-let our rooms! Tomorrow we ascend Kala Pattar to the highest point on our trek – 5545m. And we are sleeping tonight at our highest overnight – 5288m.

Day 11

Ascend Kala Pattar then trek to Lobuche

Started yearning for a bacon sandwich, fresh fruit, a hot shower and a comfy bed! Mid-holiday blues. But all dispelled as I emerge (sorry to be boring) to another cold but lovely sunny morning with clear blue skies.

Today we ascend Kala Pattar, a small mountain behind the lodge. This is not on the circuit trek, but an ascent and descent before retracing our steps to Lobuche our overnight from two nights ago.

We are at over 5000m and within ten uphill steps I am panting harder than at the end of a marathon. It is a snail's pace yet I am gasping for air. Only 50% amount of oxygen in the air compared with sea level. Slowly, slowly we plod ever upwards finally reaching the summit at 5545m the highest point in our trip after about two hours. But it is worth it. The air is crystal clear and we have a great view of Everest as well as many other peaks and the Khumbu icefall. It is spectacular. We take many pictures before starting our descent.

David Crawford

Everest

Pumo Ri

There is a group one day behind us doing the identical trek and already two members have been helicoptered out! We are feeling good and hopeful we will all finish, with an average age of 60!

We return to our lodge for lunch then return to Lobuche from two nights ago. A steady, mostly comfortable downhill trek taking about three hours.

I have a 'super de-luxe' room. But forget flat screen TV, mini bar or soft towels! Just two beds. And nothing else. But it has flowery wallpaper so I assume that makes it 'super de-luxe'.

Tomorrow is an easier day we are told. We have had three hard days so it will be welcome.

Day 12

Lobuche to Dzongla

Today is a fairly relaxed and restful day before a big day tomorrow. The weather is glorious once again, clear skies and sunshine. But by 2pm the sun is dipping, clouds are welling up and the temperature starts to plummet.

Our walk today is along pleasant paths, mostly fairly flat, though still with little uphills which leave me gasping for breath. But we have now been at 5000m or thereabouts for five days so should be acclimatising. A couple in our group are struggling with chest infections, coughs, colds and poor sleep, but these are normal for this altitude. No one seems to be suffering more

severe altitude problems. I am eating well, sleeping well and feeling good. We are still confident we will all make it.

We walk for about four hours along a glacial valley with stunning views. The pace is relaxed. We are in good spirits. And half way along the route we turn off the popular EBC trail and head towards the second of our high passes. So we are leaving the crowds behind.

We are staying in a tiny hamlet of a few single storey buildings offering lodgings for trekkers. This lodge is better than some. Still just two beds and absolutely no other furniture, but it is smaller, less busy and chaotic, and the beds have thick duvets.

A lone German female trekker arrives late afternoon seeking accommodation. She was supposed to be booked at one of the other lodges but they claimed not to have a booking. She came to our lodging but we are full also. She is concerned as she has no tent and there is nowhere else she can walk to. Fortunately our lodge offers her to sleep in the dining/lounge area. So she had somewhere for the night.

Tomorrow is a big day as we head for our second high pass — Cho La at 5420m. Wake up call will be at 5am.

Day 13

Cho La pass and trek to Thagnak

Today was a big day and hard, but excellent. We crossed our second pass, did some rock scrambling and walked on snow and ice. But more of all that shortly.

We had been warned it could be very cold overnight and in the morning. But because I have single use of a double room, I had two duvets so slept nice and warm under double duvet. In the morning we dressed for cold weather but it was cloudy, so only about zero degrees, no colder.

We had an early start, up at 5am and departed at 6am. The sun broke through the mist within an hour and we had another hot and sunny day, at least until the afternoon.

We were heading for Cho La pass. It was a steady uphill walk for a couple of hours and then a steep rocky scramble with large rocks. I enjoyed this as it made a change from endless zig-zag paths. But some in the group were less comfortable with the height and exposure. My climbing experience stood me in good stead and I was called a 'mountain goat'.

After about four hours we reached the summit (5420m) of the pass and stopped for photos. Wonderful views. We have now moved from the Everest watershed into a different valley – Cho Oyu, the sixth highest mountain in the world.

We descend from the top of the pass down a steep scramble with large boulders and stunning views of an icy glacier – not the boulder strewn moraines we encountered on the trek to EBC. We reach the edge of the glacier and for the first time are walking on snow and ice with trekking poles. It is a wonderful experience trekking on ice surrounded by high Himalayan peaks.

But all too soon we have reached the top of the glacier and are back onto solid ground and rocks. That's it for snow!

We descend to our lunch stop some six hours after leaving our overnight stop. The porters are amazing. They set up a picnic and produce lemonade, delicious soup with extra boiled rice ladled in, pasties stuffed with curried veg and boiled veg. We have a tarpaulin laid out on the ground and relax in the warm sunshine.

But we have another two hours trekking ahead so must stir ourselves and set off uphill. By 2pm cloud has swirled in, temperatures drop and the views of the mountains disappear. The altitude is still making me breathless with any extra exertion, but steady plodding gets to the top of a ridge and then it is downhill following a fast flowing stream to the small Sherpa settlement of Thagnak.

The lodge is quiet with just a few other trekkers. I have a double room again, so another double duvet night. Tomorrow is an easy day with just a couple of hours trekking.

Day 14

Thagnak to Gokyo

Today was a restful and relaxing day with just a three hour leisurely walk. We had a lie in till 7am! I won't keep repeating the weather. Just read all the previous days! It's the same.

We crossed another glacier that was a rough, rocky moraine field dotted with glacial lakes. The ice is melting and can be heard falling into the lakes. One has mini icebergs floating in it. But the overall scene is of a chaotic disused quarry rather than attractive glacial beauty. But we are surrounded by magnificent views, high snow covered mountain peaks and clear blue skies.

After a couple of hours we crest a ridge and get sight of the small settlement of Gokyo where we are staying tonight, but also the stunning sight of Lake Gokyo. A picture postcard turquoise green/blue lake nestling in the mountains. Perfection. It reminds me of Lake Louise in Canada.

Photo © S Iles

We descend to the village which sits by the side of the lake, and are staying at our best lodgings so far. Overlooking the lake, clean, large warm dining room with a big stove in the middle and gas heaters for extra warmth, clean toilets, showers, a bakery and coffee house. Wow. Almost a hotel except the rooms still have just two beds and nothing else. We have a free afternoon so a chance to do some clothes washing, enough to get me to the end of the holiday and lay it out to dry on the sun terrace overlooking the lake.

I then have a stroll along a narrow path above the lake. Looking back is the perfect scene – the lake narrows, dark hills frame the end of the lake and then on the horizon, perfectly centred is a high snow covered Himalayan peak.

I am feeling at one with nature when suddenly I see a Yak on the path dead ahead just a couple of metres away looking straight at me! I beat a hasty retreat.

Back at the lodge my washing is drying, solar charger is charging and I am feeling good. Washy washy at 3.30pm followed by tea and biscuits at 4pm and dinner at 6.30pm. Not bad.

One of our group is unwell. He has not been right for about a week and seems to be getting worse. He missed dinner a couple of nights ago and again tonight. He is taking to his bed and struggling with the walking. One of our group is a GP (Australian equivalent) so Padam (our Chief Guide) has been asking him to advise. We shall have to see if he can carry on. Tomorrow is the third and last of our high passes, so a challenging day, though there is an alternative route which avoids the pass and skirts round to our next destination. But we also have two nights of wilderness camping coming up, not ideal if unwell. Otherwise all the group are in good spirits and good health. I am sleeping well, eating well and no problems with the altitude.

Day 15

Ascent of Gokyo Ri and trek to Renjo La base

First a postscript to yesterday's post. Before dinner hot towels were brought round to the table to freshen us up. Luxury.

Today was another tough day but weather yet again perfect. Wake up call at 5.30am for an early start. We have to cross a shallow river on icy stepping stones and one of our group slips and falls in. But only sat on his bottom and got his boots wet.

Our first challenge is the ascent of Gokyo Ri (5483m) the mountain overlooking Gokyo (4800m). It is a long unrelenting lung-busting slog that takes over two hours.

But the views from the top are worth it. The most comprehensive view of 8000m peaks in Nepal. Including of course Everest. And looking down one sees Gokyo lakes (there are three of them) and the Ngozumba glacier, the largest in Nepal, stretching along the valley. We spend a while there in glorious sunshine taking numerous photos.

Next we are heading towards the third of our high passes - Renjo La. To avoid descending all the way to Gokyo and then ascending again, we turn off the path and skirt round the mountain, but on no clear path, just Yak trails, rocks and heather. An uncomfortable route but maintaining some of our height.

The plan is to rendezvous with the lunch crew. But we hit a problem – they cannot be located. The guides fan out trying to spot them and we continue walking uncertain of whether we are heading in the right direction. No phone or radio contact. Then another group of trekkers (the only ones we see on this route) are descending and say they have seen the lunch being prepared further up the trail. We continue and eventually they are found. It is unclear what had gone wrong and why, but we are now able to relax in the sunshine after a strenuous morning.

Lunch as always was good, and impressive that everything is carried up and cooked on a remote mountainside. After lunch we snooze in the warm glow of the sun before resuming our upward trek towards Renjo La pass.

An hour and a half later we arrive at our wilderness camp. A stunning setting below Renjo La, with a great view of Everest. These wilderness camps are wonderful, albeit cold as we are camping at 5130m.

Everest at sunset from the wilderness camp

We wash, have tea, take pictures then eat dinner in the mess tent huddled in our warm clothing. As we go to bed I have never seen so many stars. The sky is completely cloudless (cold night!), no light pollution and there are millions of stars visible. Amazing sight. Tomorrow we cross Renjo La.

Good news on our member who was not so well. He was dosed up on medication last night, slept well and appeared at breakfast feeling better. He walked with us all day, so hopefully should be good to finish the full trek.

Day 16

Cross Renjo La and trek to Taranga

This morning was one of those special, magical, memorable moments. But before I describe it let me remind you where we are. Wilderness camping at 5130m in one of the remotest parts of the Himalayas with the Everest range opposite us across a valley and surrounded by high peaks.

It was a cold night but I was warm in my sleeping bag and wearing extra thermals. At 6.15am a golden orb emerges from behind Everest and instantly the tent is bathed in warmth and light. It is like switching on a light. Within minutes the sun has risen above the mountainous horizon and is blazing brilliantly onto our mountainside. The air is thin and clear and pure. The sky is a perfect blue with not a cloud to be seen. Icy water droplets glisten in the sunlight on the tents. It is a moment of pure perfection that brings a tear to the eye.

The only disadvantage of having the sun so bright but so low in the sky is that it shines directly through the toilet tent, and one of our group is clearly silhouetted in the tent doing his morning business!

(You may recall I mentioned in an earlier post that another group is doing the identical trip one day behind us. Well it transpires that they opted to stay a second night at the lodge at Gokyo and miss out the wilderness camping. Now the lodge at Gokyo was nice, but to miss out on the beauty and isolation and the stars and the sunrise! Madness. I'm glad I'm not in that group.)

The toilet tent is blue and called the Blue Temple by Padam our Chief Guide. Its position at the wilderness camp was such that you could sit on the seat and look at Everest if you didn't zip up the door. I bet there are not many people can say that.

By 7.15am it is so warm and bright the dining tent has been taken down and we are having breakfast al fresco. There is something slightly surreal about the scene. Our orange sleeping tents are taken down and packed the moment we vacate them to be taken by the porters to the next night's camp. As are the porters' tents, cooking tent, dining tent etc. If a trekker had come up the trail at that point s/he would have found nine people at 5130m in the Himalayas sitting in the open air, on chairs at a table eating breakfast with no signs of a camp! (Except for the Blue Temple which is always left till after breakfast.) What would they have made of it? It struck me a Monty Python sketch could be made out of this.

Today was a significant day in two ways: firstly we crossed the third and last of our high passes and secondly from then on it is downhill all the way. We are on the homeward run.

We set off after breakfast for a relatively easy ascent to Renjo La pass (5400m) having done a lot of the hard work yesterday before camping just 370m below it. It takes about 1.5 hours to reach the pass which like the others is decorated with prayer flags.

We take photos and celebrate as we know we have done all the hard work. We have our last view of Everest and then descend the other side into a glacial valley. We are close to the Tibetan border which is the other side of the high mountains on our right.

We follow a narrow path cut into the steep side of the valley which gradually broadens and levels. As yesterday, we meet some of our porters on route who have prepared lunch. Soup, pasta, chick pea curry, home cooked flatbreads and grilled spam! We relax in the warm sunshine close to the river and a sandy beach. Yes, a sandy beach in the Himalayas.

After lunch we continue our steady descent and it is fascinating to see the landscape and vegetation and habitation change. Scrubby grass and heather are growing, we are walking on earth not rock, occasional lodgings and restaurants appear as well as farm buildings and dry stone walls. And also more trekkers, not nearly as many as on the crowded EBC route, but we are no longer in complete wilderness isolation.

We follow the river which is rushing down the valley and arrive late afternoon at our campsite for the night close to the small settlement of Taranga (4000m). But it is not true wilderness camping like last night's experience.

From the top of the pass we have descended 1400m which would be three days' uphill trekking. We are breathing more easily.

We have only two more days trekking, and talk is turning to the return to Kathmandu and the Radisson hotel! We are heading for the finishing line. All nine of us.

Day 17

Taranga to Namche Bazaar

Today is another significant milestone. We return to Namche Bazaar. We were last here 14 days ago, and returning means we have completed the main circuit of the trek. All that remains is the return trek to Lukla tomorrow for the flight to Kathmandu on Sunday.

It was cold this morning despite being at a lower altitude. The sun did not reach the camp and there was frost on the ground. We are now below the tree line, and as we descend the landscape becomes ever more green. Pine trees, juniper trees and rhododendron bushes become more plentiful. We pass tea houses and farm buildings and other trekkers. We are returning to civilisation.

We follow the glacial valley with a fast flowing river at the bottom. It is gushing and swirling with masses of white water. High waterfalls are pouring down from the mountainside. We pause at the village where Tensing Norgay used to live, and also the man who has climbed Everest 22 times – a record. Finally after a strenuous walk through woods we sight Namche Bazaar (3440m) lying below us in the valley.

Camp is bottom left

In the afternoon I wander round the many shops selling tourist souvenirs and Nepalese items. I buy presents for family, a map of the area showing the walk we have completed and change some more money into Nepalese currency. It is almost the end of the adventure.

We are sleeping tonight, as previously, at one of World Expeditions permanent campsites – so big tents, bed and pillow. No more wild camping.

Tomorrow is a 5.15am wake up call for a long but downhill walk to Lukla. It took us three days to get to Namche going uphill. Only one tomorrow for the return journey.

Day 18

Namche Bazaar to Lukla

Today is the final day of the trek. For the first time we are retracing our steps, taking one day to walk what took three days going up. Although it is a descent of 630m, it is by no means all downhill. Indeed the last 6kms to Lukla are all uphill. It is a hard slog. We are up at 5.15am for a

6.45am departure and arrive at Lukla nine hours later. So a long hard day to finish off.

We walk along a steep sided river valley with thick forests of pine trees growing up near vertical mountain sides. The river is raging and swirling in almost continuous rapids. It is called Dudh Kosi meaning 'milk river' because of its white colour. It is fed by waterfalls that flow from the highest peaks. We cross and re-cross the river on wire suspension bridges that sway and bounce as people walk across them. They hold no fear as we crossed them on the way up.

It is increasingly busy with trekkers. The trail from Lukla is the main route from the airport to all the Everest treks. So it is crowded with trekkers and yaks and mules. We pass the same teahouses we passed on the way up. They now look more civilized and smart than when we first saw them. We have stayed at far worse places higher up!

We leave the National Park and head on towards Lukla at a fast pace. Finally we pass through the gate at the entrance to Lukla. This signifies the end of the trek. We hug and kiss and shake hands. It feels emotional. We have done two peaks, three high passes and EBC. We have all completed the walk despite some sickness and altitude problems. I have been lucky and had no health problems.

We head into the centre of Lukla and there is Nepalese dancing and music in the streets. I think it is the last day of Diwali. This lodge is by far the best. We have an en-suite with shower and toilet! And there is a bedside table between the two beds. Luxury. I have my first shower for about three weeks. Heaven. We meet in the dining room and have an Everest beer. Again the first for three weeks. Clean again.

The airport at Lukla has been closed by low cloud so our flight time tomorrow is brought forward to 7am. Wake up call is at 4.30am. No lie in.

Day 19

Lukla to Kathmandu

Well, today was expected to be an uneventful post on the short hop by plane back to Kathmandu.

But, yesterday only six flights flew out from Lukla (compared with 60 to 70 in the peak trekking season). So Padam (our Chief Guide) rearranged our flight for today to be number three out, to increase our chances of getting away. This meant a 4.30am wake-up call and 5am breakfast. But bad news. No flights because of low cloud. So we waited at the hotel twiddling our thumbs, and then at 9.30am we were told we're off. The airstrip is only a few hundred metres away. We cram into a congested, cold and cramped room euphemistically called the Departure Lounge. It is packed with trekkers left over from yesterday as well as today's bookings. And we wait. A TV on the wall is constantly on an American Fight Channel showing an endless stream of boxing, kick boxing and ultimate fighting! Ugh!! And nothing is happening. Only helicopters are flying, not planes.

At 11.30am Padam took us to a nearby hotel for a coffee. We were all fairly pessimistic. If we couldn't get out today then a helicopter tomorrow would be the only option. (But at our expense to be reclaimed on insurance.) Then at 12.30pm Padam says they're flying. We all troop back to the departure lounge where there is an eager buzz of anticipation. A plane has left Kathmandu for Lukla.

The area around the departure gate is chaos. Crammed with hopeful passengers. It felt as though it would be a mad dash to the plane and survival of the fittest. A plane landed and a cheer went up. The crush and confusion increased in intensity. Then an airport official calls for 'Flight one' and people push through. Then a second plane lands, and then a third. 'Flight three' shouts the official. We force our way through the throng onto the tarmac, eager arrivals, no doubt pleased to be starting their holiday, disembark and we are on board within minutes.

The airstrip at Lukla is short, narrow and slopes downhill for takeoff (uphill for landing). The pilot taxis the short distance to the very top of the runway and turns round. Brakes on, engines up to full revs, everything shudders, and we're off.

It heads down the runway like a fairground big dipper. As it reaches the end of the runway it doesn't so much take off as launch itself into thin air as the runway disappears beneath us and we fly off into thin air. Exhilarating. The rest of the flight was uneventful apart from some cloud and minor turbulence.

Photo © P Read

Kathmandu arrivals is absolute bedlam. It is packed with passengers trying to retrieve luggage and way too small to cope. A rugby scrum. But Padam comes to our rescue and tells us to wait outside. Fifteen minutes later he emerges with a large trolley being pushed by someone else loaded with all our red bags. Into a battered minibus and we are on our way. The journey to the hotel is as chaotic and exciting as when I first arrived almost three weeks ago. Traffic is scary, motor bikes are everywhere, roads are dusty and pot-holed, small shops and businesses making, repairing and selling anything and everything line the streets.

And finally at about 2pm, having been up for nine hours, we arrive at the Radisson. A proper hotel room. Clean clothes, fresh towels, a proper shower, a big bed, drawers, a wardrobe and bedside tables. Back to civilisation.

So ends my journey. We have a day sightseeing in Kathmandu tomorrow but I will not post about that. So this is my final post (barring any major excitement tonight). Thank you for reading it. I hope you have enjoyed sharing my adventure as much as I have enjoyed writing about it. And especially thanks to those who added comments. It is nice to know people back home are with me on my journey.

So till the next adventure, goodbye.

Practical Issues

Accommodation

On my trip we stayed in three types of accommodation: eco tents, tea houses and wilderness camps. Not all tour operators offer this range, and if travelling independently or with a private guide then tea houses will most likely be your only option. Let me deal with each to help you decide how you want to travel.

Tea houses are found all the way along the EBC trail. Initially strung along the trail, and as you gain altitude located in isolated villages such as Deboche, Dingboche and Gorak Shep. In the peak trekking seasons they are fully booked, and even if you think you have a booking you may discover your room has gone when you arrive. They are busy, bustling and crowded, which is good if you want to meet other trekkers and chat about your day. But less so if you want calm and tranquillity.

The dining rooms are generally warm with a stove situated in the centre of the floor fuelled with yak dung, but the bedrooms are not heated. The food is basic but wholesome and usually has to be ordered by about

4pm. Hygiene standards are uncertain and tummy bugs are possible. Choose food carefully and avoid the water. The crowded warm dining rooms are excellent breeding grounds for respiratory infections such as coughs and colds - which can ruin your holiday. But there really is no way of avoiding them as you have to eat.

The bedrooms are basic. Think hostel not hotel. Two beds and no other furniture is the norm. Some will have blankets or duvets, which you must decide if you want to use. You may prefer to stick with your sleeping bag and drape the duvet over the top. Likewise with pillows. A useful tip is to take a clean pillow case to cover the pillow.

World Expeditions also used their own permanent eco camps, but most other tour operators do not offer this option. An eco camp is a campsite set up for the trekking season on land rented from a local house or lodge owner. The tents are large enough to stand up in and have a metal frame bed and pillow. Eating is in a dining room in the house and there are outdoor toilets.

I found the neat layout of the tents a bit sterile, reminiscent of a Scout camp or even a UN refugee camp. But I preferred them to the tea houses. You were not eating in a crowded dining room with up to 100 other people, although at Namche Bazaar there were five World Expedition groups, so perhaps 50 or so people. But at other places it was just our group of nine. The facilities were better than for most tea houses, and the cooking is done by World Expedition cooks, thereby minimising the risk of food poisoning.

The third type of accommodation, and for me by far the best, was wilderness camping. The tents and all the equipment are carried to the campsites which, as the name suggests, are in remote areas away from the crowds of trekkers. The tents are smaller, you sleep on a thin mat (unless you bring your own camping mattress), there is no pillow and eating is in the unheated dining tent, not indoors with a yak dung fuelled stove.

But you are in the most beautiful and remote settings, with no other trekkers and the view from the tent is glorious. It will be cold at night, as the wilderness camps are at high altitude; but wrap up warm and settle into your sleeping bag and you will be fine. The toilet is a hole dug into the ground, but with a toilet tent and a seat on a metal frame. In many respects, preferable to some of the dubious toilets in the tea houses, or indeed in the eco camps.

Health Matters

Let me start with a disclaimer. I have no medical qualification, so my thoughts in this section are based on my own experience, advice received from other people or information gleaned from the internet. If you have any medical doubts or concerns you should consult your own doctor. Trekking in Nepal is challenging (especially on the higher routes) and you need to be fit and healthy at the outset.

The biggest concern is altitude sickness. Fitness or youth are no guarantee of protection. Indeed, there is a suggestion that younger, fitter trekkers are more likely to suffer. But this may be because they are over-confident and set off walking too quickly. 'Slowly, slowly' is the constant refrain. Train hard, but walk slow is sound advice.

The best protection against altitude sickness is acclimatisation. You should not aim to ascend more than 500m in a day, and should take a rest day at around 3000m and another at around 4000m. A rest day means you sleep two nights at the same altitude, but you do not rest during the day. Instead, you climb higher and stay at the higher altitude for a few hours (ideally) before returning to your overnight stop at a lower altitude. This is another mantra: 'Walk high, sleep low'.

With this acclimatisation schedule, most people should suffer little more than minor symptoms such as headache, fatigue, loss of appetite, shortness of breath or a dry cough. You should drink plenty of water, no alcohol, avoid strenuous exercise for the first 24 hours and eat a high calorie diet.

Far more serious (but fortunately far less common) is Acute Mountain Sickness (AMS). This is a medical emergency and can lead to death. AMS can lead to High Altitude Pulmonary Oedema (HAPE) which is fluid on the lungs, or High Altitude Cerebral Oedema (HACE) fluid on the brain. Symptoms of HAPE are: blue tinge to the skin, breathing difficulties, tightness in the chest, persistent cough and difficulty breathing. Symptoms of HACE are: headache, nausea, vomiting, confusion and loss of co-ordination. The treatment for either condition is to get down to a lower altitude immediately and bottled oxygen if available.

If you are travelling with a reputable tour operator, they should have access to a Portable Altitude Chamber. This can be described as a strong plastic chamber which fully encases the casualty and is then pumped to a higher air pressure. As a result the casualty is breathing air with a greater density of oxygen than the prevailing atmosphere. Our guide has had cause to use it twice in 10 years. So it is not a frequent occurrence, but it's nice to know it's there if needed.

Diamox (Acetazolmadide) is a prescribed medication designed to help prevent altitude sickness and treat it if symptoms do arise. It may be available from your GP, or if not from a travel clinic. The NHS website recommends it for prevention. You should start a couple of days before going to altitude and continue for at least a few days afterwards, or until descending below 2500m. But there are differing opinions.

The arguments against taking it as a precautionary measure are that you may get side effects, and if AMS does develop then it is not available as a treatment. The compromise advice is to take it at half dose for prevention, which reduces possible side effects and means the option to increase to a full dose is still available if symptoms develop.

This is the tactic I adopted both in Nepal and on my Kilimanjaro trip, and I did not experience anything beyond very mild altitude symptoms on either trip. Of course, I have no way of knowing how I would have been without Diamox. The most common side effects are tingling in the fingers and toes and increased frequency of urination. I experienced only minor tingling, but nothing discomforting or painful; and increased frequency of urination, especially at night.

Diarrhoea and vomiting (a tummy bug) following dodgy food or water are problems which can spoil your holiday. This is another benefit of using an established tour operator who will often provide their own cooks or supervise the preparation of meals under hygienic conditions. Eating at tea houses is more risky.

Do not drink the water anywhere. Use only bottled water for brushing your teeth and if taking a shower avoid getting any water in your mouth. Carry a small bottle of hand sanitiser with you at all times and use regularly, and always after visiting a toilet and before eating. Choose your foods carefully. Eat only fruit which needs peeling (e.g. banana or orange), not one which has been washed. Avoid salads and even be careful with cakes and bread as these are made with water and may not always have been thoroughly cooked. Vegetables are safer than meat or poultry. And take a supply of Imodium with you; and toilet paper!

Khumbu cough is another commonplace ailment. Named after the region of Everest where it often arises, it is a high altitude hack caused by low humidity and temperatures. Almost everyone who spends time at high altitude will develop this. For most it is irritating rather than disabling. Drink plenty of water, suck on a sweet or throat lozenge, wear a Buff or balaclava and try to avoid over-exertion (though easier said than done if trekking at high altitude).

Colds and respiratory tract infections are also quite frequent. The body's defences are weakened at altitude, and the tea rooms are crowded with trekkers and with little ventilation. They are a fertile breeding ground for infections. If you are staying in tea rooms there is little you can do except try and keep yourself as fit and healthy as possible and hope your natural immunity will stave off any infection.

Look after your feet. If you develop blisters or other problems with your feet, your trek can become a painful nightmare and you might not be able to continue. Hopefully it should go without saying, but I will say it anyway: take boots which are well worn-in, comfortable and have not given you any problems on long multi-day treks. One of the people on my trek had 30 year-old leather boots which had never given him any problems. He was loathe to buy new ones in case they were not as good. Stick to what you know and trust.

Wear good quality socks. Do not stint on these. Bridgedale or Karrimor are not cheap, but worth it. You should wear clean socks every day, which means regular washing and drying. Some people prefer to take silk inner socks for warmth, for protection and because they are easier to wash and quicker to dry than wool socks.

I washed my feet every day at the end of the walk and then massaged them with fellwalkers peppermint and eucalyptus foot lotion before putting on clean socks for the evening, and to sleep in on cold nights. The next morning I removed the socks to put Vaseline on my toes before replacing the socks for the day's walking. I did not suffer any problems. Take a supply of Compeed blister plasters and use them at the first hint of rubbing. Do not delay. Once a blister has formed it can be painful even when protected.

Communications

You may like to get away from the world for the duration of your trek and have no contact with the outside world; or you may want to post pictures and updates on social media every day and keep in touch with friends and family back home.

WiFi is available along much of the main EBC route. In places such as Namche Bazaar there are cafés offering free WiFi for the price of a cup of coffee, though it can be variable in speed and reliability. Some of the lodges have WiFi for a charge, about £3 for 24 hours. And a new service is now available from a Nepalese company called Everest Link. It offers

WiFi at multiple locations on the route to Everest - and reputedly on the summit itself, though I was not able to check this out! You buy a card for £4.20 with a username and a password you reveal by scratching off the surface, and this buys you 20mb of data. You can use it at any location where you pick up the network.

The other problem is keeping your phone charged. Most lodges offer a charging service for about £3.50, but I took a solar charger. Reviews of solar chargers often express disappointment, but I took a three panel Anker PowerPort, and it worked extremely well. I did not need to pay for a charge at any time. In bright sun it would charge from dead to 100% in about three hours. In cloudy conditions it still worked, though more slowly. It has two USB outlets, and others in the group were using it to charge their phones or cameras also. It makes you popular for one reason at least! I either wore it draped across my rucksack when walking, or hung it on the tent on arrival at camp.

Toilets

I have been to Glastonbury twice, so am used to toilets that are less than salubrious; and I know Nepal is a Third World country so its standards may not be as high as expected by western Europeans. But nevertheless, you need to be prepared that the toilets anywhere on the EBC trail can be pretty grim. Some toilets are western style with seats (of sorts), others have the traditional 'starting blocks' where you need to crouch.

Above about 4000m, because flush cisterns would freeze in winter, you have to use a jug dipped into a large plastic drum to obtain water to flush the toilet. Nowhere provides toilet paper, and nowhere can you flush toilet paper, so a bin in the corner accumulates a rather unpleasant pile of used toilet paper.

In some of the tea houses there is just a hole in the ground with a small brush to sweep dirt into the hole once you have finished. So don't go trekking in Nepal if you are squeamish about such things. Take your anti-bacterial gel to use immediately after you have finished, as well as washing your hands - if there are any facilities for this.

And whilst on the topic of toilets, let's deal with the issue of needing to go in the night. This was a regular topic of discussion on our trip, because it is quite a problem. It is cold at night, possibly very cold if high up, the toilets are not lit, and even finding them in the dark can be a challenge. The zips on the tents are noisy, and if sharing a tent your companion will be woken up. Not to mention dogs or yaks lurking outside your tent. If you are taking Diamox (a side effect of which is increased frequency of urination) you may well be going three or four times in a night! So wear your clothes in bed, have a torch and shoes handy, and prepare for exiting the tent and returning as quietly as possible; and remember which tent is yours! Even if staying in tea rooms, you need to leave your room, find the toilet and use it in the dark. Not always easy.

But the best solution is to take a container with screw top, and use this at night. This is what I did and it was an absolute lifesaver. You can get up and pee and be back in your warm sleeping bag within a minute. In the morning the container is emptied, rinsed out and a supermarket plastic bag pushed inside as a liner. The container can then be stuffed with clothes for transport to the following night's location, thereby taking up minimal space in your bag.

However, if you are sharing a tent you need to negotiate with your companion. Not so bad if you have travelled together, but altogether more tricky if sharing with a stranger. Another good reason for paying a single supplement to have your own tent or room.

Shopping

There are shops all the way up the route to EBC, so if you have forgotten something or run out or lose it, don't panic. All the essentials you might need are available. In the larger villages such as Lukla and Namche Bazaar there are tourist shops galore selling gorgeous hand-knitted blankets, shawls, scarves, hats and gloves in rich Nepalese colours at very reasonable prices. As well as more touristy gifts such as yak bells. So you can browse on your way up and buy on your return.

The shopkeepers are not pushy, unlike other countries where you will be pulled into a shop and not allowed to leave unless you buy something. They hope you will buy, after all tourism is their lifeblood, but they are a more reserved and polite people and will accept that you may wish to look and leave. Respect their culture and show courtesy in return, even if you choose not to buy. Appreciate their goods and thank them for their time and service.

Beyond the main towns and villages you will find roadside stalls outside houses or even just spread on the ground at the side of the trail selling hats, jewellery, scarves and other items. Browse and buy if you fancy something. Prices are reasonable and the people friendly.

Negotiating a price is expected, especially for gifts, less so for staples such as soap or toilet paper. This is always a conundrum for more reserved Brits who are less comfortable with bargaining. Especially so when the prices are generally already very fair and the people are not rich.

Around the tourist hotspots in Kathmandu, you should expect to bargain robustly. The hawkers will be more forceful, contrary to my earlier comments. So in Kathmandu, near a popular tourist site, I was offered a necklace for 2000NPR (about £14) and bought it for 300NPR (£2.10) as I was about to step onto the mini-bus to depart.

But outside of Kathmandu, and on the EBC trek route, the sellers are less pushy and the prices more reasonable. For example, in Namche Bazaar I bought gifts where the total marked price was 6500NPR (£45.50) and I paid 6000NPR (£42). But for this I got a deliciously soft 100% yak wool blanket, two scarves, three hats and an adorable Nepalese jacket for my 16 month old grandson. All for £42. Not bad.

Remember, it is a poor country which has suffered political turmoil and natural disaster. The people are warm, friendly and polite. If we share a small amount of our Western wealth with them it does us no harm and helps improve their quality of life. Be generous and don't bargain too hard.

Tipping

Tipping of the guides and porters is expected. Although it is labelled optional, it should be considered as part of the cost of your trek (unless you have really had problems and are seriously dissatisfied). But normally, you will not begrudge it once you have seen how hard the porters and guides work. How much to tip is the question.

With a larger group on an organised trek with a tour operator you will be advised of the recommended range. The going rate (in 2017) was 600NPR (£4.20) per person in your party per day for all the team (porters, cooks and assistant guides) except the Chief Guide. On an 18 day trek with nine people in the group we jointly tipped 99,000NPR (£700) to be split between 20 people. Our Head Guide dealt with the exact division of the money, as there is an established hierarchy, with the Head Cook, for example, receiving more than the porters.

The Head Guide should be tipped separately, and not in front of the rest of the team. Courtesy and respect are important in Nepalese culture and it would be disrespectful to include the Head Guide within the overall tipping for the rest of the team. We tipped 6000NPR (£42) each for the Chief Guide, making a total of £380 in round figures.

People are then free to make individual tips on a personal basis if any of the porters or guides have been particularly friendly or helpful. But again, this should not be done in front of anyone else.

If you are hiring a guide independently then there are likely to be less of you in the group, and no Head Guide to split up the amount between porters and others, so you will have to take more responsibility. But the amounts are about the same as above. You will not a have a cook as you will be eating in tea houses, and possibly just a guide and two porters if you are a small party. A suggested price for tipping is one day per week of the trek or 15% of the price you are paying.

Take some envelopes to put the money in rather than displaying it openly, as this can be seen as disrespectful and lacking cultural sensitivity. And tip in the local currency of Nepalese rupees, otherwise you create problems, and possibly cost, in exchanging foreign currency. Tips to the porters might be given on the penultimate night as they disperse the following day once the gear has been carried down. So don't rely on getting to a cash machine on your last night, you need to have the money before then.

There is also a tradition, though less expected than tipping, of leaving any spare, unwanted or older clothing or shoes for the porters. Indeed, some people bring clothing from the UK for the explicit purpose of donating. Don't worry if you have been wearing it for a week, or trying to decide if it will fit a particular porter. There seems to be an exchange system, so even if a particular porter does not need a jacket, he will exchange it for donated shoes for example

Kathmandu

Whether you are trekking in the Everest or Annapurna region, you will arrive and depart via Kathmandu and probably spend a day or more there at the beginning and end of your trek. As with the rest of my advice, this is not a comprehensive tourist guide to the city, but merely my impressions and reflections.

For people of my generation who were growing up in the sixties, the name Kathmandu has a mystical, magical ring that is perhaps hard to appreciate now. The Beatles travelled to nearby northern India to study transcendental meditation under Maharishi Mahesh Yogi. Hippies travelled to Kathmandu in search of spiritual enlightenment with The Krishna Consciousness Society. They fell in love with the city, its people, freely available drugs and the counter-culture lifestyle. They embraced its values, religions and rejection of Western materialism.

But it didn't last. In the mid-seventies, the US government, no doubt feeling threatened by this alternative perspective on the world with its rejection of capitalism, directed the Nepalese government to regulate the inflow of tourists and control the free use of drugs. The hippie numbers dwindled as they sought enlightenment elsewhere. Nevertheless, this image is imprinted in the minds of children of the sixties.

Today it retains little of this unique, counter-culture lifestyle, though remains popular with backpackers, trekkers and gap-year travellers. It is not a city you would want to spend long in. It is noisy, busy, dusty, vibrant, bustling and clogged with traffic. The trip from the airport into town is an eye-opener for those used to first world countries.

The bumpy pot-holed roads are thronged with traffic, yet a cow can be found lying in the middle of the road with cars and bikes swerving to avoid it. There are no pavements, just dusty sidewalks lined with tiny businesses and shops selling, making and repairing everything and anything. People are everywhere sitting, talking, walking and standing. There is energy and activity. Although a poor country, it does not look impoverished. There is not the extreme poverty one hears about in India, for example.

The city centre is more developed with a mixture of modern buildings interspersed with older and more dilapidated ones. The electrical wiring is a sight to behold and amaze. Thousands of wires are draped from post to post in a spaghetti-like tangle. It is hard to believe how anything can be transmitted through such a mess. Yet presumably it works.

The traffic is another cause for astonishment. Cars and even more so motor bikes are everywhere. There seems to be a loose rule of the road to drive on the left, (frequently ignored) but otherwise there appears to be no logic, rhyme or reason to govern which vehicle has priority or how intersections and junctions are to be negotiated. There are hordes of motor bikes, often carrying more than two people or with a young child standing on the footplate or laden with goods. At first it was bewildering, yet after a couple of days a certain order could be discerned.

Imagine a busy railway station concourse with passengers moving in all directions to and from the platforms, and entering and exiting at various points around the station. There are no 'rules' to govern pedestrians' behaviour except common sense, courtesy and you don't just barge into someone else. Everyone understands this and more or less obeys these unwritten rules. Everyone crosses the concourse in safety at a steady pace, pausing occasionally if someone passes in front, veering left or right to manoeuvre round a group of people and sometimes spotting a gap which allows a brief increase in pace.

Well that is how the traffic in Kathmandu seems to operate. Everyone heads broadly in their direction of travel, at a steady pace, mostly without road rage or much sounding of horns, manoeuvring around vehicles and allowing others to proceed if they are ahead. There is none of the frenetic driving found in Rome or Istanbul, and none of the shouting or gesticulating you would get in the UK if you pulled out directly in the path of another car.

It works because everyone plays by the unwritten rules. I did not see any scrapes whilst there, even though cars are moving within inches of each other and on all sides. However, at rush hour the sheer volume of traffic does overwhelm the roads and police with whistles (and face masks against the dust and fumes) attempt to impose some degree of order and traffic management on the chaos.

And crossing the road works on the same principle as traffic flow. There is no point waiting for a gap in the traffic or for a car to allow you across, even if standing on a zebra crossing. You will wait for ever during the rush hour. Nor should you try and spot a gap and make a mad dash to the other side. This sudden movement will be unexpected by drivers and riders and risks a collision. (Think back to my station concourse example. You would not try and sprint across the concourse because you would almost certainly crash into someone. Well the same applies to crossing the road.) Instead you walk steadily out in front of the traffic which will either move behind you or in front, or stop if no alternative, but without any hooting or fist waving. In this manner, you calmly and serenely take your life in your hands and just walk steadily to the other side. And mostly it works!

You should visit the district of Thamel, indeed you may be staying there. It is the commercial and tourist centre of Kathmandu, and became the focus for the hippies and artists who started visiting some 40  years ago. Some people describe it is a ghetto, and complain it is dirty, unsafe and too touristy. But many more consider it the place to be, especially for the budget-conscious traveller.

It is around a square kilometre of narrow alleys, crowded with all kinds of shops and cottage industries, cheap hotels and restaurants. But beware of the cars, motorbikes, taxis and even rickshaws which travel on most of the  streets, though a few are thankfully traffic free. You can buy food, fruit, vegetables, all manner of trekking gear (some genuine, most copies of brand names), rolls of cloth, clothing, souvenirs, handicrafts and pretty well anything else. It has a wide range of mountaineering and outdoor shops, foreign money exchanges, mobile phone shops and pubs and clubs.

Reviews say it has been cleaned up over recent years and is better policed. Certainly when I was there I felt completely safe (during the daytime, I didn't visit at night) apart from the traffic, and it was no more dirty or dusty than the rest of Kathmandu. I found it vibrant, exciting, fascinating and entertaining. Even if you don't want to buy anything or eat there, do visit to wander the streets, and marvel at the ingenuity of people who find so many ways to make a living by running a tiny business or shop or restaurant. If you don't like Thamel you probably shouldn't be visiting Nepal.

There are many other tourist attractions to visit, but some of the main ones are:

- Boudnath: One of the largest Buddhist stupas in the world

- Pashupatinath: A Hindu temple on the bank of River Baghmati and site of cremations

- Durbar Square: site of the Royal Palace as well as temples.

- Hanuman Dhoka: An old royal palace

- Swayambhunath: Known as the Monkey Temple

I visited only the first three, but a Google search will quickly give you more information on the others if needed.

Stupas are to be found throughout your trek in Nepal, but **Boudnath** in the centre of Kathmandu is worth a visit for its size and grandeur. The surrounding buildings are intricate and ornate.

The fluttering prayer flags are quintessentially Nepalese, as are the lines of prayer wheels. In galleries in the square around Boudanath you can see students learning the art of painting mandalas. A mandala is a spiritual and ritual

symbol in Hinduism and Buddhism. In its basic form it is a square with four gates surrounding a circle, and this pattern can be found on many items in Nepal. The paintings are extremely intricate and colourful. You can purchase if you wish, or just admire

You can also experience a singing bowl. This is a polished metal bowl which is placed on your head or other parts of your body such as your back, and struck gently with a padded stick. The metal bowl resonates with an undulating singing

Photo © S Iles

noise which is supposed to have healing powers. When I tried it on my head it made my whole brain vibrate in an uncomfortable fashion. I had to stop it within a few seconds. Others seemed to find it quite pleasant, but whether it heals you must decide. Not for me.

The most fascinating visit for me was to **Pashupatinath**, a famous sacred Hindu temple on the banks of the Bagmati river 3kms north west of Kathmandu. It is one of the four most important religious sites in Asia for devotees of Shiva, and the largest temple complex in Nepal.

But it was not the buildings which captivated my attention but the human activity. It is a cremation site where the last rites of Hindus are performed before the body is cremated on an open funeral pyre. Visitors watch curiously from the opposite bank of the river, hawkers sell trinkets and monkeys roam freely.

It feels unpleasantly voyeuristic as a Westerner to be observing and photographing the grief of families washing and then burning their loved ones. Funeral ceremonies in the UK are conducted privately, with solemnity and discretion. Yet here, the families are lining up with their dead wrapped in orange burial shrouds, crowds of relatives are watching and some wailing, the body is washed on the edge of the river and then cremated in full view of a crowd of tourists. It was both entrancing and uncomfortable in equal amounts.

The body is manhandled to the water's edge (it is not carried serenely by pall bearers as would be the case in the West) where various relatives douse themselves and the body in the holy (but highly polluted) waters of the Bagmati river. The emotional intensity rises amongst the women, dressed in white the colour of mourning, whilst the men do the more practical task of moving the body.

After ritual washing, the body is carried to one of the concrete plinths on the edge of the river where wood and straw have been placed in preparation. The pyre is lit and the body is cremated in full view of the family and the onlookers. It burns for hours and eventually the ashes are swept into the holy waters of the river. A relative then enters the water to retrieve some of the ashes, though it must be impossible to know what is being retrieved from the murky waters. There is not just one ceremony taking place, but multiple ones lining up by the river bank and then along the line of cremation sites. Unsettling to watch, but also enlightening to see how different cultures deal so differently with death and grieving.

Here you will also see strangely dressed Sadhus (holy men) sitting cross-legged posing for pictures. Traditionally, a Sadhu was a religious ascetic who renounced all worldly goods and dedicated his life to meditation and contemplation. They survived on gifts from the public and once they had enough to survive for a day accepted no more.

Photo © S Iles

But sadly, in tourist hot spots they have become a tourist attraction and will invite you to take photographs and pose with them, but for a price. It reminded me of street artists at the Edinburgh festival. Incredible make-up and costumes, but in the end just providing tourist entertainment to earn money. It spoils the illusion of a true ascetic.

Durbar Square is the generic name to describe the plazas and areas opposite the old royal palaces of Nepal. The square in Kathmandu includes temples, idols, open courts and water fountains. Sadly the earthquake of 2015 has damaged many of the fine old buildings as is evident by the bamboo props supporting the cracked and tilting walls.

Tourists must pay 1000NPR (£7) to enter the square and temples, but as I had little time I just observed from around the perimeter. It may be better if one has the time to enter the temples, but I found it disappointing compared with some of the other sites on offer.

But after a couple of days you will be ready to depart Kathmandu having had your fill of noise, dust, bustle and traffic. And head off on your trek or home.

Postscript

The most frequent question I was asked on my return was: 'What's the next adventure?'. It seems sad in this fast-paced world that people always want to look to the next experience rather than fully embracing the moment. A trip such as this takes time to absorb. It needs reflection and integration.

It taught me that age need be no barrier. The trip requires health, fitness, confidence and personal resilience. But if you have these, then in the words of the well-worn cliché, age is just a number.

Nepal is a beautiful country. The mountains are awe inspiring and beautiful. The rocky glaciers are equally awe inspiring, but brutal and rugged, looking like a disused giant's quarry, with stones, rocks and boulders piled on each other in a haphazard and chaotic fashion.

EBC confirmed my fears. It was busy on the trekking route, sometimes crowded, and tea houses and shops accompanied it much of the way, especially at lower altitude. The Base Camp itself (at least in Autumn when there are no expeditions preparing to climb) is no more than barren glacial rocks with nothing to commend it. Only the lines of prayer flags and a small hand-written sign on a piece of rock differentiate it from the miles of similar rocks surrounding it. (And the crowds of trekkers.) But in the end, it is EBC, and if that's what you want to see then you need to do this trek. But if you want to admire the mountains, get away from the crowds and experience the true beauty and wonderment of Nepal, you will do better elsewhere.

The people were friendly, courteous, reserved and calm. Meeting them helped to rebalance the materialism of the Western world. Perhaps we could all learn a few lessons from them to appreciate the true value of life. Let's hope the influx of tourists and trekkers with their money does not change them for the worse.

Printed in Great Britain
by Amazon